The United States of Europe - 2066

The Importance of Playing Cricket

by

Ian Goult

A novella set in the London region of the state of England, previously part of the United Kingdom of Great Britain, during the millennia of the last successful invasion of that state,

It deals with the interaction of two final year students and their interaction with an ambitious EU Commissioner and his scheming wife.

A vision of the future, but less surreal than George Orwell's 1984, and perhaps more realistic!

First published: 2016

Issue 2: 2017

Copyright © Ian Goult

*ISBN 9781546377030

Published by Ian Goult

PREFACE

This story is fiction, written by one of the common people, a voter, proclaimed by the politicians drafting and setting in concrete The Treaty of Rome, believing themselves to be above "the rest," arrogantly setting up a regulative structure of Commissioners to have greater wisdom than the voting public; who may not be conversant with macro or micro economics, but can see when something is not right - laws able to override both existing national law and any future laws; enforced by the EU Court of Justice (EU-speak for EU Court of Law). Who did they turn out to be?

Many thoughtful people studying deeply the contents of the Treaty of Rome declared it flawed; and as the common people see, so it has turned out; inflexible and set in concrete, taking no account of a future that might, and did, develop away from traditional concepts.

It is emphasised that it is the author's observance that is the scope of this book.

An appendix has been added. as "The Observations of One of the Common People."

The current issue is post Brexit.

CONTENTS

Introduction:

INTRODUCTION

It is said that the observer can see more of the game than the participants and it is emphasised that it is the author's observance that is the scope of this book.

Many thoughtful people studying deeply the contents of the Treaty of Rome declared it flawed; and as the common people see, so it has turned out; inflexible and set in concrete, taking no account of a future that might, and did, develop away from traditional concepts.

The purpose of this story and comment is to present a future scenario and comment; as such it is deliberately contentious.

During the run-up to the referendum on Brexit it was claimed that it was unfair to the younger generation to be denied the advantages of membership to the European Union; the author, refraining from voting on the basis that it was not for a 92-year-old to influence the future of the up-and-coming generations, believes that the opposite is true. The new generation showed its metal at Rio, and should be free of the binding diktats of the EU enshrined in the European court of justice (Euro-speak for law).

CHAPTER 1

Two Final Year Students

Fred Howard ducked as one of the arrows fired by the Normans under William the Conqueror came straight for his eye. He looked sheepishly to his left to meet the eyes of the girl, who he had barely noticed before, all students tending to look the same in loose fitting tracksuits. She and all the rest of the students in the dome had all ducked at the same time. She held his glance for a moment, then burst out laughing. He grinned, trying unsuccessfully to hide his embarrassment.

"I've had enough of this," he said. "Care to join me for a drink?" he added hopefully; for he had noticed she was quite attractive. Beneath her neat white track suit, he surmised, was a very trim and lithe little body. She had a face that was pleasant rather than pretty, with a retroussé nose, slightly freckled. Her fair hair was cut short, as was the fashion with young people, with a lock falling casually over her forehead. She wore no make-up - she didn't need to. She smiled. She had a lovely smile.

"I'd love to," she said. "My, it's really hot for October."

"Thanks to those idiots sixty years ago who tried to pretend global warming didn't exist."

They made their way to the exit carefully avoiding the fallen British, one of who had an arrow sticking in his eye.

"I always felt sorry for Harold," commented the girl. "It seems he was just plain unlucky"

"No. He made an error of judgement. He should have bided his time, allowed William to come further inland, where he would have been more vulnerable, and his own troops rested from their long march from the North where they had just repelled a Scandinavian invasion."

"You seem to know all about it."

"History's my thing."

As they reached the exit there was a series of blood curdling yells from behind them as the Normans charged at the now defeated and fleeing British.

"Phew, that was too near real reality for me," said the girl as they made their way to the outside refreshment bar in the leisure complex. Fred ordered two mixed fruit drinks, flashing his identity ring, with its small circle of stars, at the detector to have the transaction recorded on the Colossus, colloquially known as dump, derived in turn from the popular press's domc, after naming the massive mainframe computer and data storage system in Brussels the Doomsday Computer. The Brussels Colossus was linked to a Mini-Colossus in each of the European regions. Between them every item in the Union was recorded, whether a house (with all occupants), school (with all pupils), pub, warehouse (with all transactions), church, animal (domestic or farm) or person. Every transaction, however trivial was recorded.

Had Fred ordered an alcoholic drink the barman would have received a warning that alcoholic drinks were forbidden for students. Had the barman served an alcoholic drink a criminal offence would have been recorded against both Fred and the barman. A debit fine would be imposed automatically.

They took their drinks to a riverside table. "I'm Sally," announced the girl, "reading Engineering at University College Europe (London Region). I'm in my final year."

"Pleased to know you, Sally. I'm Fred; in my final year too, Economics at The European School of Economics, just down the road from you."

"I thought you said you were reading History."

"It's really Economic History…"

"Like the Battle of Hastings," laughed Sally. Her laugh was infectious. He laughed again remembering the corny super 3D plus virtual reality replay of the invasion by the Normans, which had been compulsory for all students to attend on the fourteenth of October, the day of its millennium - significantly in the many times refurbished millennium dome. His attendance would have been detected as he passed into the building and duly entered onto his record in the mini colossus.

"No, not like the Battle of Hastings; contemporary economic history, illustrating the great advances that have been made since the formation of the European Union."

"Do I detect a note of scepticism?" There was a mischievous gleam in Sally's eyes. They both laughed again.

"Look, it's a glorious day," Fred said. "There are better things to do than discuss economics. What would you like to do for the rest of the day?" He looked hopefully at Sally.

"Let's go to the South Bank. There's a more interesting celebration there," she said.

"A Hundred Years of Pop Music; should be interesting. It was supposed to have originated in the swinging sixties of the last century with a group known as the Beatles. I reckon it was earlier than that: 'started with Dixieland Jazz half a century earlier, followed by..."

"Anything you don't know?" enquired Sally.

Fred reddened. Confused, he stammered: "Damned know-all, aren't I." He saw her eyes were more mischievous than mocking. "I'd love to go." This was an understatement. He could have said that he would like to go anywhere with her full stop. "I'd like to take you to the River Boat restaurant afterwards."

Sally looked doubtful.

"Don't worry, it will be on me," Fred added quickly.

"No. You must be on low credit yourself. I do know what it's like. I try to be frugal; but I'm in a debit situation. There's no need to go to an expensive restaurant. There's time to go back to the college refectory for a snack."

"OK. If you're happy with that we'll catch the next cable car."

They did not have long to wait. The twelve-seater overhead cabs passed every three minutes, dipping down to pick up passengers at every designated stop along the main thoroughfares. There was just one change from Greenwich to Gower Street, as there was from Gower Street to the South Bank

The cable cars ran swiftly above the streets, radiating out to suburbia from central London, crossing five radial rings centred on the old city. There was always a stopping point where a radiating arm crossed a radial route, as well as several intermediate stops on the outer rings. At every cable stop there were mini electric taxis for the short distances to roads not served by the cable cars. The ageing underground system served to take the overflow at peak periods.

With the exception of those residents in the metropolitan area no cars were allowed. One car per resident within the area was permitted. It had to be a gas/electric vehicle using battery power in the metropolitan area, reverting to gas power between urban areas. When under gas power the batteries recharged, ready for entry into another electric power only urban area. Those travelling by car from outlying districts had to leave them at the many 'park and ride' points around Greater London, using either the overhead or underground system. Electric cabs and minibuses were also available with parcel, pram and invalid carriage space. Road freight with deliveries within the metropolitan area could use gas-fuelled engines. No through traffic was allowed.

"It really is a lovely evening," Sally said as they left the European Festival Hall after an evening of old time Disco dancing. "Let's cycle back. They made their way to the cycle racks and chose their respective mounts, punched in the reference numbers on the terminal keyboard and flashed their identity rings at the infrared sensor to release the bikes. They mounted and moved off in the designated two width cycle lanes, chatting happily, disturbed only by the occasional electric taxi and the whirring of the overhead cable cars and a few impatient cyclists calling for them to get into single file to overtake.

It was quiet as they cycled over Waterloo Bridge. They fell silent, catching the mood of the river, now at full flood, reflecting the bright streetlights from either bank. Before they reached the end of the bridge Sally dismounted and leaned her bike against the side-wall. Fred followed. Sally was looking down into the River. She said, without looking up:

"I don't want to go back to my flat just yet."

Fred said nothing. Flat? Most students had lodgings. Without looking up she continued:

"I've had a row with my boy-friend." Fred's heart sank. Row or no row, there was a boy-friend. There always was. Rows could be made up. His fiancée had ditched him during his second year, but not due to a particular row, of which there had been many. She simply wasn't prepared to hang around in Hereford until he had completed his degree. She moved in with a local farmer, became pregnant, and since European law, and thus the Colossus, didn't acknowledge single mothers and unmarried fathers (unless legally separated or divorced) were criminals, they were now married.

"I'm sorry," he said. She gave him a wry smile. She knew he was smitten, he realised. She was being frank with him. He liked her for that. "Well I am sorry," he added. "But I wouldn't have met you otherwise and I am pleased about that."

"Me too," she said. "I've enjoyed the day. I didn't expect that. You made me laugh.

John - that's my boy-friend - would have been furious if I had laughed at him."

"So I might see you again?"

"That would be nice."

CHAPTER 2

Students at Play

"Fitness is an essential complement to work, or in our case study," said Sally

"Sounds like a sound bite from the system," said Fred.

"It was. I just added the study bit, and I happen to believe it."

Fred had no doubt about that. It was mid-morning and they were in the nearly empty bar at the Fred Perry Indoor Sports Centre, so named in 2038 to commemorate the hundredth anniversary of the last English Wimbledon champion.

It had been Sally's idea that they should join an independent club rather than play at the University sports Centre, and Fred had been happy to go along with it. It was where they always met. They had formed a formidable doubles partnership, playing for the premier team at the centre. She was light on her feet, fast and agile. They had no set strategy, but a natural empathy, each anticipating the others' movements. Their relationship followed the same easy casual fashion. Fred was careful not to push it beyond that. The thought of John in the background was continually on his mind, but he knew that she would broach it in her own good time. She broached it now.

"You've never asked me about John since we first met."

"No."

"You hoped he would just go away."

"Yes"

"Well he hasn't."

"Tell me all about it."

"Sally paused. "I first met John during my first year at college, the first term in fact. There was the usual socialising; everyone was new. It was an exciting time. I seemed to attract a lot of attention."

"I'm not surprised," murmured Fred.

"John was head and shoulders above the rest - literally, he is very nearly two metres, a hundred and ninety centimetres in fact."

"Six foot two," grinned Fred.

"Shut up. I'm being serious."

"Sorry."

"As I was saying; not only was he tall."

"He was tall, dark and handsome."

"Yes. He also seemed more mature than the rest. He played rugby for the university and the London Region, sometimes going on international tours."

"Quite a guy."

"As you say. Quite a Guy; and knows it - bags of charisma - full of confidence. His parents are both big in Brussels. His father is a Commissioner. His mother is of German origin, and both languages are used within the family, so John is naturally bilingual and studies French and Italian as part of his political studies course. He is obviously being groomed for the very highest office. He is used to hobnobbing with his parent's high-ranking friends. He already thinks of himself as one of them. He created quite an impression on me." Sally paused, looked intently out of the window.

"He was also used to getting his own way," she said.

"I understand."

"He still wants his own way, or perhaps I should say, his Mother's way."

"How come?" asked Fred.

"Oh dear. It's all very difficult."

"You've got a sympathetic listener."

"I know." Sally paused. "I used to think that John was the most arrogant person in the world - until I met his mother. She idolises him. He can do no wrong - unless he thwarts her will.

She's also the only person who can dominate him; and she does."

"You've met his mother?"

"Yes. I spent the last two Christmases at his home - his South England home. They've a luxury flat in Brussels as well. Their home in South England is a refurbished manor house, which doubles as an office for both of them. The stables have been converted, or rather rebuilt, into an office block. Each has their own office suite staffed from Brussels; they include catering, housekeeping and general maintenance personnel."

"Sounds impressive."

"Very impressive; I was impressed. John said how pleased he was that his mother liked me. I was over the moon, and I was made to feel welcome; very welcome in fact, particularly last Christmas, when Mrs O'Conner, that's John's mother, told me I could look upon their home as my home. Every time John visited his parents I went with him."

"John has his own flat, but lived mostly in mine. This saved him from catering and general maintenance - not that many of the other female students wouldn't have willingly taken my place. We'd lived as a couple; but I thought when I told him I didn't want to see him again and locked the door against him that would be the end of it. I hadn't allowed for his mother."

"What the hell's his mother has to do with it."

"Everything. She had decided that I would make a suitable wife for her son."

"Too bad."

"John had the nerve to tell me he wanted to make up because that was what his mother wanted. After I told him what I thought of that. I heard from his mother. She 'phoned to tell me what a wonderful life I would have with John and I would be stupid to turn him down again. I forgot to mention that I had already turned him down once, saying I wanted to graduate first. This resulted in a lecture on how unimportant graduation was compared to the standing I would have as John's wife. In fact, I was already having doubts. The hospitality was just that little bit overdone. The natural warmth was missing. I was the privileged wife-in-waiting, a necessary appendage to John's future career."

Sally gave the ghost of a smile. "This time I told her I couldn't stick her John at any price; but when I began to tell her why she stopped me dead and told me to come and see her."

"Why?"

"Pornography."

"Pornography?"

"You know that any word associated with pornography or paedophiles trips the inspectorate alarm."

"Yes, of course," said Fred, "that massive crackdown on the proliferation of porn and similar evils; drugs, the lot. I can imagine the furore if they were visited by the Inspectorate."

"The media would have a field day. The inspectorate comes under Mr. O'Connor. He's very proud to be responsible for one of the biggest bunch of officials in Brussels. Strange; he's quite a nice man. I liked him better than Mrs O'Connor."

"It's a pity he doesn't have to deal with his damned officials," murmured Fred, "It was their constant interference in my father's business that brought about his early death. There were more inspectors telling him how to run his business than he had staff to run it. Anyway, what was it that would have sullied their untarnished reputation?"

"How about attempted Gang Bang Rape?"

"Sally?"

"Yes. I could hardly believe it either."

"You don't have to tell me."

"I need to tell someone. I accept that the odd drunken orgy is part of rugby lore, and as such I was prepared to put up with it from time to time. But about a week before I met you the London Region team returned from Paris having beaten the Paris region against all the odds. John came back to the flat with a few of his team-mates. They'd been celebrating their victory at the club in Twickenham, where the drinking rules had been relaxed for the occasion, and were already pretty drunk. They started singing lewd songs and drinking again - a situation I had had to put up with on many occasions before."

"I was in the kitchen making coffee, hoping to sober them up a bit, when one of them shouted, 'what about a gang bang Sal.' I would have expected my boy-friend to have rebuked such rudeness. But oh no. 'Yeah, strip off Sal' he said, lurching towards me. 'Let's be having you.' Fortunately, he was so drunk that I had no difficulty in running to my room and slamming the door before he could reach me. I slammed the bolt to and pushed my bed across the door. They hammered and jeered for a bit before returning to their drinking. I sat up shivering and crying all night."

Fred put his hand over hers.

"When I went down in the morning the place was a tip. John and his pals were sprawled all over the place. There was vomit in and around the sides of the sink. I called a mini-taxi and told his shamefaced pals to clear off. I demanded an apology from John, but he denied everything and called me a prissy little bitch. I piled his belongings in a bag, threw it out of the door, and told him I never wanted to see him again. He flounced out saying he was through with me."

The bar was beginning to fill. There were tears in Sally's eyes. Fred pressed her hand. "Let's leave here," he said. "I'll take you home."

"No. It could get you into trouble."

"How could taking you home get me into trouble?"

"Because of a visit by John's mother, when she stopped me speaking on the 'phone and demanded I went to see her at her home I ignored it. So yesterday the mountain came to the molehill. She came to see me."

"That must have been a nasty experience."

"It was. She was in London attending one of her many committees."

"QUANGOS"

"QUANGOS, including the University Inspectorate Board. When I told her what happened she said I was being petty; it was natural that youngsters should let their hair down occasionally. It was just a bit of harmless fun. That did it. I threw caution to the winds." Sally looked up at Fred and smiled at the recollection.

"Do you know," she said, "All my pent-up thoughts and doubts about John and his high powered family came out in my tirade. I didn't know I had it in me. I told her what I thought of her idea of harmless fun; especially in view of the high moral tone she and her husband's apparatchiks take in public, kowtowing to the churches when I knew from their attitude that their God was the system and their prime concern the maintenance of their position within it. I added for good measure that I had no wish to be important due to the person I married, only just managing to stop myself actually saying 'as she was.' To my surprise, she heard me out in silence; saying, very quietly, 'you have one more chance to make it up with John. You should know from what you have just said which side your bread is buttered.' This morning I had notice to quit my flat."

Fred said: "My rooms are rented privately. They are cramped, but room could be made for one more. In the meantime," he said looking at the rapidly filling bar as the daylight was fading outside; it's time we left here. I take it you have a period of grace before you are on the street."

"One week. But there's something else. John let it be known that anyone messing with any girl of his had better watch out"

"Am I supposed to be scared?"

"Fred, he's...he's bigger than you."

"Get up Sally. I'm taking you home."

Sally returned his steady gaze, got up, and they left the bar.

CHAPTER 3

The Commissioner's son

John sipped at his second can of lager as he lounged with his feet across the front seat of his electric car. It was parked opposite Sally's flat in a grubby little cul-de-sac off Upper Gower Street. His casual attitude did not reflect his state of mind. He was not used to being dumped by a girl-friend, let alone one who, he now realised with hindsight, was the girl he would really like as his wife. In short, he missed her. A call from his mother hadn't helped. The tirade of stinging abuse was still ringing in his ears. His friends added to his discomfort.

He had just left a meeting at his flat to discuss the New Year's rugby fixtures. Present were the captain of the university team, James Stuart, the vice-captain, Pete Melbourne, and the fixtures secretary, Samuel Smith, a jovial black fellow, nearly as tall as John and as effective in the line out. John didn't like Sam. He knew Sam could replace him in the regional team, and it was the regional team that got all the media publicity. John loved that. Sam took a delight in goading John. John hated that.

John's flat in a secluded mews off Gloucester Terrace was chosen as the meeting venue, being spacious and being outside the university premises - it was owned by John's parents, had a good stock of lager, forbidden in the university. As the meeting broke up Sam yawned, closed his fixtures book, and decided to break the monotony.

"I hear you've lost your girl-friend," he ventured.

"I chucked her," responded John, not at all pleased.

"Yeah - a lovely girl like Sally," Sam mocked.

Pete, who had been at the drunken fracas in Sally's flat, intervened. "What would John want with a prissy little cat like that," he said.

Sam had liked Sally. "Of course," he said, "I should have realised, tarts are more in your line." It was pointless denying what was already well known.

Pete scowled at Sam. "You're too damned self-righteous for your own good," he said. "Perhaps you fancy your chances with Sally."

Sam broke into a broad grin. "Yeah, I'm whiter than white," he said, easing the tension that had built up. "And as for Sally, opportunity would be a fine thing. Maybe I'll cut you out John."

"I wouldn't fancy the chances of anyone crossing John." James said. "I'm surprised he hasn't had a go at you already."

"He's scared of the race relations inspectorate," smiled Sam.

"There's no difference between races anymore," snapped John. "We're all Europeans now."

"And that's official." Sam said.

"So what's official about Sally then?" James turned enquiringly to John.

"Nothing," replied John, and thus the meeting had broken up.

Left on his own John moodily concluded that he had made a mess of it. He would go to see Sally again and although it went against the grain, admit he had behaved badly and apologise. It had been a mistake to mention his mother's wishes last time. It was his wishes that mattered.

Sally wasn't at home. He'd wait. That should flatter her.

He'd finished his second lager before he noticed two people approaching. He jerked upright in his seat as he saw it was Sally with her arm linked to her companion to whom she was having an animated conversation. The last thing he wanted was a third party to his apology, but he couldn't avoid it. She would recognise his car. She did recognise his car, and the look on her face was anything but welcoming. She slipped her hand into Fred's and gripped it tight as John got out of the car.

John ignored Fred. "Sally," he said, "I really would like to apologise for the other night. Could I have a word with you."

"No. Can't you see I'm with a friend?"

John looked at Fred as if he had seen him for the first time and with a voice oozing with disdain said, "And who may you be?"

"Is there something wrong with your hearing? Sally told you. I'm her friend. Now step aside and let Sally into her flat. She said she didn't wish to talk to you."

"Who the hell are you, telling me what to do?" John sneered, not moving.

"The name's Fred Howard. Now move aside, you drunken slob." John's face went purple with rage as Fred stepped forward.

"John don't...." screamed Sally as John made as though to knock Fred off his feet. This was a mistake. Fred who had practised the noble art in his school days anticipated what was coming and swung away leaving John temporarily unbalanced. Fred shot out his left fist straight into John's solar plexus with all his weight behind it winding him and doubling him up. Fred was now able to swing his right fist hard up into Johns face. For good measure, he followed it with a quick left hook as John staggered back against the door, blood oozing from his nose. John paused with his back to the door, eyed Fred as a bull might eye a red flag and charged forward head down to come at Fred with a rugger tackle. He had learned nothing from his previous experience, for Fred, instead of retreating lunged forward, crashing his fist into John's jaw. John's legs buckled from under him and he fell to the pavement.

"My God, you've killed him," Sally gasped kneeling down beside John's prostrate body.

CHAPTER 4

A Spot of Bother

Steward Roy Rush and Steward Pauline Temple of the University Inspectorate were on foot patrol. It was early evening and they were not expecting very much activity.

The University Inspectorate was a small sub branch of the London Metropolitan Region Inspectorate. The two stewards were from the local office specifically responsible for checking compliance with the laws relating to the running of the university, that were many, including security and maintenance of law and order within the university area. Stewards were generally police cadets in training for full status as inspectorate police. Inspectorate police, as the name suggests, were an amalgamation of the police and inspection bodies of the European Union, so formed to streamline the comprehensive task of monitoring and enforcing regulations governing every activity from manufacture of clothes, baking of bread, forging of steel, growing tomatoes, education and leisure activities; and, of course, crime. A policy of zero tolerance together with the monitoring of every activity of every individual and organisation had enabled the virtual elimination of petty crime, drug smuggling and drug abuse.

Stewards did not have the full powers of the inspectorate police, who could charge and log an offence on the Colossus enabling initiation of the appropriate punitive and corrective action. Only if an appeal against the reported offence was lodged would a case be heard by the Regional Court of Justice, or one of the subsidiary district courts. An appeal could only be lodged if there was lack of corroborating evidence of the offence, or if it conflicted with any of the defined rights as laid down in the European Bill of Rights.

Pauline was thrilled to be assigned to the university branch of the inspectorate since she heard that her younger brother's sporting hero, John O'Connor, was a student. She had taken no interest in rugby, or any other sport until she happened to be in the room where her brother had been watching the London-Paris match on virtual reality television, and they interviewed John, who had played a leading role in London's victory. His fine features and languid air of confident authority worked their magic. She was hooked. She fantasised over all the press cuttings she collected off the Internet. One day she was sure she would meet her hero.

The two stewards were walking towards the upper end of Gower Street. Roy was talking football. Roy talked of nothing else but football. In this he was not unusual, for football took pride of place in the news media. Other sports had their place of course; but it was football and its personalities first and foremost, then the other sports. There was little interest in other news. Current affairs were covered, but were so rarely accessed that they had to be subsidised by The Commission's education budget.

Roy asked:

"Why are you so interested in rugby. Football is much more interesting."

"Nicer people play rugby."

"Rubbish." Roy played football for his area team, as well as supporting Queens Park Rangers, and was somewhat put out.

"You've been assigned to crowd control. Football crowds are a rowdy drunken lot. It seems zero tolerance goes out of the window when it comes to football hooliganism. I heard it rumoured that the authorities turn a blind eye to football rowdiness, believing it to be a sort of safety valve. Better to scream and shout abuse at each other rather than at the authorities."

"What a load of rot."

Further discussion was cut short by a shout of fear from round the next corner: "No John," followed by a scream, then; "My God you've killed him."

Rounding the corner at a run, their actions were instinctive. Pauline knelt down beside John, whilst Roy grabbed Fred by the arm.

"What's going on here then?"

Fred, somewhat surprised by the sudden turn of events, said reassuringly: "Don't worry. I didn't hit him all that hard. He'll come-round shortly."

As if on cue John stirred, groaned and started to raise himself.

"No," said Pauline placing a restraining arm on his shoulder, removing her cap and placing it on the ground and gently eased his head back onto it. John looking up at the concerned face of a very attractive police-cadet, instinctively gave her the best smile he could manage from his very painful face and complied. He needed time to think.

Pauline was looking into the face of her hero. He'd been hurt. She pulled out the antiseptic wipes that she always carried in her side pocket for just such emergencies, gently wiped his forehead and bruised face, and cleaned the blood from his nose and chin.

"He jumped me," said John, now fully aware of the situation. "It was an unprovoked attack."

Sally, as soon as John stirred, had got to her feet and turned to Fred. She froze. The pained expression as his eyes met hers had nothing to do with the steward gripping him by the arm. She barely noticed him. "No, Fred. I went to John concerned for you. Fred darling..." She wanted to hug him. She heard John's accusation and whipped round.

"You lying swine," she screamed. She turned to the steward holding Fred.

"Let him go," she said. "That brute on the ground went for him."

"That's the not the way it looks to me," the steward said retaining his grip on Fred's arm. "The one that got hit is plain for all to see."

"But you didn't see. I did. I tell you that that thug down there took a swipe at my friend as he attempted to stop us going into my flat."

"And landed up on the ground with a black eye and a bleeding nose," sneered the steward, a likely story."

"I had to defend myself," Fred said trying to shake his arm free from the steward's grip only to find it gripped even harder. "When attacked by a rugby wing forward it's no good using half measures."

Rugby wing-forward? Roy, football enthusiast though he was, recognised the now fully conscience young man getting to his feet. He remembered too that much had been made in the recent press coverage that John O'Connor was the son of a Commissioner. Furthermore, Roy knew that Commissioner O'Connor's responsibilities covered the Directorate of Police. "You will be pressing charges, sir?" he enquired turning to John."

Sally gave a wry smile at this and turned her gaze to the corner of the building. She knew there was a security camera there, as did John who had noted the direction of her gaze. Sally wasn't sure if the camera covered her door, or just the main street; nor was John.

"Not worth bothering with," John replied nonchalantly, turning to Sally. "Perhaps I could go into our flat to have a clean-up Sally, and talk to you now. This is all so very upsetting. I know you hate violence."

"You've got a nerve," replied Sally "I have already told you I don't want to set eyes on you again; but perhaps now we have representatives of the police here my friend and

I can gain unmolested entry into my flat." Sally looked enquiringly at the two stewards, and addressing John again, adding: "and if you don't move your car you'll collect a parking fine."

Pauline started towards the car and turning to John said: "Why don't you come back to our office for a tidy up. You can leave your car in our compound." The other steward looked none too pleased. "I'll continue with our patrol," he said."

"And your colleague will finish up as a Chief Inspector." said Sally opening her flat door."

Once inside the door of her flat Sally flung her arms round Fred. "Oh Fred, Fred darling, what have I done to you," she gasped.

For answer Fred placed his lips firmly over hers and pulled her closer to him. She lingered in his arms for a while before shaking herself free. "Don't you see," she continued, "I have ruined you."

"I don't see how," he said leading her to the sofa, and sitting down beside her with his arm round her shoulders. "I've just done what I have wanted to do ever since I met you. And as for John, you know he won't bring charges. If that security camera caught the action think what the tabloid media would make of it. He'll persuade that young lady copper to forget it. From the look in her eyes he could persuade her to do anything."

"And probably will," added Sally. "But Fred, you've got to take it seriously - do you want a lager by the way, there's some in the fridge?"

"No; but a cup of hot strong sweet tea would go down very well."

Sally jumped up and went into the kitchenette. Among the rattle of cups and saucers she called, "this flat was a sort of grace and favour flat. It was allocated to me after my first year. Who was I to query it? Now I'm out of favour. What will happen next? The great Madame O'Connor has turned her fury on me covering anything or anyone connected with me; and now you will be seen to be linked to me."

Fred got up and went into the kitchenette.

"That's the way I want it," he said, coming up behind her and enclosing her in his arms.

CHAPTER 5

The Commissioner

A lavish life style had never been an ambition of Commissioner O'Conner. It just happened as a side effect of his position. Politics had been his passion since his student days at the European School of Economics. His tidy analytical mind was fascinated by the structure of the European Union. He was certain it could be improved by the application of more rigorous controls.

He set about obtaining a position in the Brussels' technocracy. Within the Directorate of Transport he masterminded the radical overhaul of the transportation systems within urban conurbations throughout the Union. The zeal and dogged determination he showed in pushing through the necessary legislation made him a household name throughout the Union. It was not surprising, therefore, that following the major upheaval when the European parliament showed its authority for only the second time since the reforms of the early century and dismissed the entire commission for consistently failing to root out the corruption and mismanagement that was endemic to such a centralised authority, that one of the newly appointed commissioners should be Peter O'Conner; appointed, furthermore, to the powerful Inspection Directorate, which was given extra powers to audit and investigate departmental spending. It seemed to Commissioner O'Connor's tidy mind that the overlap between the inspectorates' investigations and police investigations in bringing wrongdoing to book, created administrative conflicts and indeed jealousy between the two functions, and argued that bringing them together under a single authority, namely his, would create a far more streamlined, effective, and cost saving activity. This accorded with the mood of the new political outlook and was readily endorsed.

One of the first to recognise the potential of Peter O'Connor was his first personal assistant Clara Braun, who wasted no time in making herself Clara O'Connor. The change from being his invaluable assistant and supportive wife to a thorn in his side took about twenty years. She was addressing him now.

"It's about time you did something about that son of yours," she said from across the room, or rather the virtual room, for he was in Brussels and she was in Surrey. He sighed;

John was always 'his' son when there was trouble. "It's no good looking like that. You know you have never showed the slightest interest in him." Never been allowed to you mean, he thought, but said:

"What's the problem?"

"You're the problem. You've never been a proper father to him and taught him how to behave." True, he was pampered from birth. "And now he has split with Sally."

"That is a shame. Can't they make it up?"

"Both John and I have tried. She has another boy-friend. He seems to be a thug. He went for John when John was trying to speak to Sally. Then when I went to see Sally to try to make her see sense she was extremely rude to me. I'm having her turned out of her flat. You will have to do something about that new boy-friend of hers. I've already found out who he is and looked at his record in the personal data bank; it's clean, but there is a record on the movement file of attending the Australian Lobby meetings."

"You have no right to access my data files."

"I'm your other half. Remember? Are you or are you not going to support me? I have already persuaded the college to add 'a record of violence' to his college report. This was witnessed by two stewards. You should have him put under surveillance. The files showed his father complained that he had to close his business due to excessive interference from the Inspectorate. His son probably feels aggrieved. Such people can be subversive and students, as you know, can get particularly disruptive. His name, by the way, is Frederick Howard."

"But..."

"Just do it." The room disappeared from the wall. Peter O'Connor wished it was in his remit to dis-invent some inventions. It was not even in his remit to get involved with operational procedures; but to define policy. Clara was well aware of this. He rang the Director General - Operations.

"Is that you Poirot, he asked as the familiar rotund and moustachioed face appeared on the video screen."

"It is, Peter. What can I do for you?"

"It has been brought to my notice that a student at one of the London Region Colleges is a potential trouble maker. I don't know any specific details other than his name - Frederick Howard. He should be put under surveillance."

"I'll get the regional superintendent onto it immediately. By the way, Louise and I are having a few friends to dinner tomorrow. We would be very pleased if you could find the time to join us."

"I'd love to. Unfortunately, I have an appointment in Strasbourg tomorrow. Some other time perhaps."

Strange, thought Poirot, the courts were in recess. Not much else went on in Strasbourg since parliament had been transferred to Brussels, and why should the Commissioner take an interest in a particular individual, unless perhaps it was to do with the Australian Lobby the old British regions' media had been making so much of recently: Not that much could be done about that. Freedom of speech was enshrined in the Bill of Rights; and that made it easy to keep abreast of popular trends. Nevertheless, it was a pity they didn't give more prominence to their recent abysmal sports performances. Shrugging his shoulders, he rang the Chief Superintendent - London Region. He also contacted the Chief Superintendent at Strasbourg.

CHAPTER 6

The Australian Lobby

"This is superb, Sally. I can't remember when I last had a full English breakfast," Fred said, tucking in with relish to porridge, followed by bacon and eggs, sausage and tomato, toast and marmalade. They hadn't bothered to eat the previous evening.

"You've forgotten the porridge part," said Sally, pointing to the packet showing a muscular kilted athlete throwing the Hammer."

"OK, British breakfast. Have you Scottish ancestors?"

"I have. On my mother's side." Sally sipped her tea; she too had enjoyed her breakfast. "Have you any lectures today?" she enquired.

"I have; but I'll give them a miss."

"So what is our plan of campaign? I know it's ridiculous, but I feel a sense of exhilaration now that battle is joined."

"You can't beat the system you know."

"No; but being on a hiding to nothing gives you wonderful freedom of action. It isn't natural for students to be submissive and compliant. The system puts us in a straightjacket. Comply or else. It's blackmail. It's as if we didn't have minds of our own. You can't beat the system; but you can kick it."

"We can start by joining the Australian lobby. As you think I might suffer character assassination as an uncontrollable thug I can lose nothing by conforming to their label."

"OK. I've heard a bit about it. Fill me in." Sally moved to the sofa, tucked her legs up and rested her head on Fred's shoulder.

"It means going back a bit in history."

"I'm listening."

"It stems from the isolationism of the Union. It can be argued, with some justification, that keeping aloof from military conflicts in other countries has given the citizens of the Union just on a hundred years of peace and comparative security. The India Pakistan conflict was an exception."

"But we kept clear of that," said Sally.

"Yes. Wisely in the event. I was talking of the follow up. The loss of life and total devastation following their nuclear exchange was so mind boggling that neither the United States nor ourselves could brace themselves to face up to it. In the anarchy that followed China stepped in. Using draconian measures, they managed to bring some sort of order out of chaos. They are now in a similar position in India to the British a couple of centuries ago. This is no bad thing as far as we are concerned. The problems facing the Chinese are on a scale that will need all their resources, keeping them fully occupied and out of the international arena for decades."

"Continuing the background to the Australian lobby we come to the rest of the Far East. Following from years of petty wars and revolutions that were more of interest to the Americas than us, they viewed the European Union, and with the encouragement from America formed their own Union, the Confederation of Pacific States. Due to the disparity of the member states it outlines common purposes rather than attempt full compatibility. Their treaty is more flexible than ours."

"You mean more sensible."

"I mean more sensible. But due to the huge area covered even this only became possible with enhanced information technology and virtual reality. They have a parliament without a parliament building."

"I know all about that," said Sally. "I have a project to outline the software to generate similar committee arrangements based on the model of the Pacific Parliament. Each member sits at his desk in his own country or region, seeing themselves as sitting in the virtual parliament with all the other members sitting at their desks, arranged in a semicircle around the speaker. The speaker can call on any member to address the chamber in the normal way. It's fascinating. I ought to be getting on with it now."

"To-morrow darling," said Fred. "Returning to the Union of Pacific States, this posed a problem for Australia and New Zealand. Should they or should they not join the confederation. If they joined there would be some common purposes that they would find difficult to swallow. A referendums in both countries there was an overwhelming majority in favour of staying out."

"I remember. John's father was discussing it last Christmas. He seemed to think it could create problems."

"It has. The Confederation looks to the vast open spaces of Australia to relieve its overpopulation problems. It has published plans to bring vast tracts of land into cultivation based on the methods used to vegetate the desert areas of North Africa."

"And what it can't get one way it will get another," said Sally

"Exactly. It's only a threat at the moment. However, the Australians are seeking assurances of support for their continued sovereignty from both Europe and the USA. The USA are sympathetic and are giving verbal assurances and moral support that falls short of a formal offer of material assistance against possible aggression without a similar commitment from Europe. Europe doesn't want to know."

"Except for the Australian Lobby."

"Yes. The Lobby is confined almost exclusively to the English-speaking part of Europe, the old British Isles. Even here there is apathy, but there is also a groundswell of opinion swinging towards it. It is beginning to alarm the Commission."

"When can I join?" Sally asked.

CHAPTER 7

Emille

"We are the new courtesans," said Emille, in English.   Her English was better than Commissioner O'Connor's French. "You are the new aristocracy."

"Except that we can be voted out of office," responded the Commissioner.

"Better than the guillotine. But you live dangerously with me."

"Who would betray me?"

"Not me.   The courtesans knew their place in the hierarchy. We know our place in the system - outside it. The French understand these things. The British think differently."

"So why am I here?"

Emille smiled. "You tell me."   She swung her shapely legs off the bed and slipped a housecoat over her naked body.

"Because you are adorable. You are irresistible. You have become part of my life. I could not continue without you."

"Pah!   If it was not me it would be someone else."

"Never. Only you can criticise me, say the most outrageous things and get away with it."

"Your wife criticises you?"

"And I resent it."

"Ah, mon Cherie, I believe I really do love you." She bent down and kissed him on the forehead. He would have pulled her towards him again but she slipped away into the bathroom. "It's too late to go out," she called. "I'll cook up something here."

Peter sighed, picked up his towel and went into the shower room. He had picked the location of Emille's flat carefully. It was directly above his own modest flat in Strasbourg; a third flat he needed in case he had late meetings at the courts. This seldom happened. He considered it a convenient bolthole. He was considering it as he finished the delicious salad Emille had just knocked up, as only the French knew how.

"You know," he said, "I'm a hypocrite."

"But an honest hypocrite."

Peter laughed. "Only you," he said, "could make such a contradiction in terms. Who ever heard of an honest hypocrite?"

"I have. Who else would admit to being a hypocrite?"

"It's self-evident. Why not admit it - not in public of course. I was appointed to wipe out hypocrisy and double-dealing in government. I am seen as a hard man, a puritan above reproach, a scourge to clean up the system and root out sloppy administration."

"And you have succeeded, my poppet. A man should be judged on his achievements. His private life is nobody else's business."

"There's the paradox. I am the darling of the churches and other bone fide religious bodies. I've posed as their friend, licensing them to protect them from rival unorthodox pseudo religions. For the good of the community as a whole I have been able to take draconian measures, allegedly to wipe out pornography and organised crime, restricting and monitoring the internet to limit its use only for approved purposes; but again, giving my inspection directorate access to any activity they wish. I'm a clever sod"

Emille laughed. "You should be careful," she said. "It sounds as though you have a conscience. That's bad if you wish to become the next President - as seems likely. A conscience and ambition don't go together."

"I'll have to watch my conscience and try to keep it in check."

"You'd better, Commissioner Bridgette Crouton's more ambitious than you, and she's got no conscience. She is hoping to become the next President, and she's very close to President Heinrich Cripp. He makes no bones about naming her as his probable successor."

"And she's more photogenic than me."

"For heaven's sake, it's not a beauty contest, and in anycase you are still a fine figure of a man. It's not as if the electorate had any say anyway."

"The electorate, or rather the media on their behalf, influence the regional MEPs who now select the President, and by the time of the election Bridgette Crouton will have been disgraced. I am biding my time."

Emille smiled. "Crafty bastard. All those rumours about her junketing all over the world and profligacy of her Foreign Affairs Directorate, not to mention her life style. They are the softening up process are they?"

"What mischievous thoughts."

"She can be pretty crafty too. How else did she get to her position, and she is a little too close to the president for comfort."

"She's all sound bite and no substance, like the rest of them."

"Oh, Peter love," laughed Emille, "you do have a good opinion of yourself."

"For good reason, you little minx. I am the only Commissioner capable of getting the system to function efficiently."

"Is it functioning efficiently?"

"No. That is why it is important that I am the next President. I have a record of success in transport, and law and order. It's time I brought industry under tighter control. I can only do that with the full authority of the presidency. It needs tighter control from the top. Everything needs tighter control from the top."

"Rubbish."

"Pardon."

"I said rubbish, and meant it," Emille continued. "You forget I was the secretary and occasional interpreter for the steering committee tasked with the development of the domestic and commercial virtual reality plus-plus. The European version that was initiated and vastly over funded to be the first with the best never really got off the ground. It finished up last and worst, just as the European effort at the turn of the century to produce high definition television using old analogue technology failed. The lessons of history are always ignored. We finished up adopting the American system of digital virtual reality."

"Your own transport system," continued Emille, "used the overhead system pioneered in Japan."

"That is exactly the reason for tighter political controls. This is my main argument for my adoption as president."

"It takes one of the common people, a mere copy typist and part time interpreter, to prick the bubble of your grand design."

"You forget the most important qualification - mistress to a European Commissioner."

"Correct. You would never deign to listen to a mere copy typist, one of the common people. You can only dictate to them."

"Strong stuff! OK, mere copy typist, prick my conceited bubble."

"It wasn't the ineptitude of the research and development teams that caused projects such as the virtual reality plus-plus to fail. It was continuous meddling by the politicians on the steering committee and the jealousies of the multiregional project offices each fighting to get the most prestigious slice of the cake. The designers were frustrated by the cumbersome administrative machinery. In other words, the designers needed space. They can't work with administrators looking over their shoulder all the time and querying every minor setback. The politicians monitoring the project in reality have very little they can contribute, but have to justify their position. In engineering design by committee is disastrous. When the committees are headed by politicians it is catastrophic."

"So how do you control industrial development?"

"Look to history. Were Marconi or Henry Ford controlled? Their motivation was the will to succeed - to achieve for its own sake. When I was in the United States collecting data on the virtual reality project I visited the Smithsonian Museum. I saw an interesting report from the late nineteenth century documenting in detail the government sponsored attempts to achieve flight by heavier than air machines. The Wright brothers achieved it on a shoestring. I doubt if they had committee meetings or issued progress reports."

Peter met Emille's eye. "I want to achieve the perfect state," he said.

Emille put her hand over his. "You are doomed to failure," she said.

"I am not in the habit of failing."

"Then this very ordinary person had better warn you."

"This should be interesting. I'm listening."

"That should make you unique among graduates of the European School of Economics who are not noted for the habit of listening - only of pontificating, especially on matters on which they have no experience."

"And you think I have no experience?"

"Not of the real world. The world most of us live in. You went straight from college to Brussels. You speak as though running the EU is no different to running a large grocery store where everything has its place and everyone knows their place.. A military style of leadership is applicable. It can run like a well-oiled machine."

"That is not a fair statement Emille. I am surprised at your naivety. Of course I realise that the EU is a multi-disciplined system. A system for which knowledge of economics is essential. I have that knowledge and background."

"There you have it." responded Emille, "A multi-disciplined system. There are people in that system. They are not cogs in a machine. Nor are they willing or wish to be cogs in the machine, to be told where their place is, and what they should do in it. This is where communism failed, a fine ideal to be forced on people for their own good. You can only make it work by becoming a dictator. A cog that doesn't fit has to be discarded; or worse, reformed to fit."

"Good God, Emille, you make it sound as though I wish to become a dictator.

"What else will achieve 'greater control from the top? Your words, not mine. Good governance follows wise delegation."

"Perhaps it is you that should be running for President."

"Oh, Peter, my love, I'm only trying to warn you. I don't want you hurt. And watch that Crouton woman. Make sure you're not discarded."

Peter laughed. "I'm seeing her tomorrow," he said.

"What about?"

"Cricket."

CHAPTER 8

The President

On entering Commissioner Crouton's office Peter O'Conner was surprised to see the commission President, Heinrich Cripp seated at the opposite side of her massive oak table. He swung round in his chair as Peter entered and gestured to a seat at the end of the table. Peter addressed them in German, a language in which all three were proficient."

"Good morning Mr President, good morning Bridgette," he said.

Bridgette made the slightest acknowledgement with an inclination of the head.

"Good morning Peter," said the President. "I have joined Bridgette this morning because I share her concern over the growth of the so called Australian Lobby in the regions of the former UK. This is an informal meeting to agree a policy to put to the whole Commission."

"Indeed! You surprise me. I see no need for your concern or for a policy. Free speech is enshrined in the EU treaties. They are only expressing an opinion."

"Free speech - yes," said Bridgette. "However, we are talking about an Association. That is illegal. It is an unregistered society. What do you intend to do about it?"

"Nothing," said Peter. "It is a Lobby not an association or society. There is no legal reason why it should not exist as a pressure group. It is peaceful. It's not actually doing anything."

"Now you surprise me Peter," said the President. "You are playing with words. That's not like you."

"No," said Bridgette, "you didn't concern yourself with names when your inspectorate police cracked down on paedophiles and similar groups,"

"For heaven's sake what are you two driving at? They were criminal groups."

"Exactly," snapped Bridgette, "Isn't plotting against the Union a criminal act?"

"There is no evidence of plotting," said Peter. "It is not in my remit to crack down on free speech and I don't intend to do so even if you don't like what is being said."

"What is being said is damaging to our foreign policy and trade. That is an action against the State," said Bridgette. "Our trade with the Far Eastern Bloc is comparable with that of the Americas and far in excess of anything we do with Australia and New Zealand."

"Aha, now we have it," said Peter. You would see Australia sacrificed for the benefit of our trade."

"Why should we concern ourselves with a large but comparatively insignificant country on the other side of the world," said Bridgette. "There is no threat to us."

"They didn't say that when the Europe was overwhelmed by the Nazi war machine - I have chosen my words carefully, Mr President. They came to the aid of a country the other side of the world at great sacrifice to themselves. The Australian Association is not even calling for a sacrifice, but simply for a show of solidarity with the United States and Canada. The United States no longer has the relative influence it used to have"

"Foreign policy is my province, not yours," said Bridgette. "I suggest you leave it to me."

"Law and order are mine," said Peter;" so why are you telling me what to do?"

"We are advising you," said the President. "As President that is my prerogative."

"Then I suggest you advise Commissioner Crouton to be a little more circumspect in her pronouncements," said Peter. "This is the reason I made this appointment to see her in the first place. Perhaps you missed the media headlines of a few days ago."

"I noticed nothing unusual," said the President."

Perhaps you are not interested in the sports section as are the majority of the general public. You would certainly ignore it if it had to do with cricket."

Bridgette burst out laughing. "Oh Peter, are you really that sensitive? Can't you take a joke?"

Peter went to the wall console and dialled up the appropriate headline:

COMMISSIONER CROUTON ON THE
AUSTRALIAN LOBBY

"WHAT DO YOU EXPECT FROM A PEOPLE WHO PLAY CRICKET"

"You think that a joke," continued Peter. "You are concerned with the growth of the Australian Lobby. The joke is on you. At a stroke, you have increased the membership by several million. In the English-speaking regions every town, every suburb and most villages have at least one cricket club. Each club has between a couple of dozen to several thousand members. The reaction to your stupid remark is that virtually every club has allied itself to the Lobby. I hope you are satisfied."

"Oh Peter my love," laughed Emille, on his return "I never realised you played cricket."

"I don't get a chance to play much now," Peter said. "I was captain of my school team and am Honorary President of the Godalming and Rural District Cricket Club. Those two clowns Cripp and Crouton want me to dissociate myself from cricket."

"And you will defy the President of the European Union?"

"No. Ignore him."

"So! What is more important; your ambitions or your cricket?"

"I obtained my present position as a Commissioner by dedication and hard work. The Presidency of the cricket club was an honour bestowed on me by the club members. I would not insult those who so honoured me. It would be no good explaining that to Crouton and Cripp. They don't understand cricket."

"Neither do I," said Emille. "I am only just beginning to understand you."

CHAPTER 9

Poirot

Poirot Anderson, the Director General of the European Police Inspectorate, was a hard taskmaster; diligent and conscientious himself, he expected the same from his subordinates. His dedicated approach to his work had propelled him to the top; or nearly to the top.

"I could become a Commissioner next year," he said to his wife. "Peter's recommendation, which he has promised, would be enough to enable me to replace him if he becomes President. Alternatively, I could disgrace him now and replace him sooner."

"How could that be?" asked Louise. "I thought his integrity was unassailable."

"That is the image and it makes his downfall all the easier. Mild indiscretions are accepted as the norm, except for those who are above reproach. He and his wife adopt a high moral tone."

"His wife in particular."

"Exactly; How would she react if he had a mistress?"

"Oh no! I can't believe it. Peter with a mistress, anyone else, but not Clara's husband. Tell me it's true."

"It's true enough. It was Clara pushing her husband to use the police inspectorate system for personal malice that set me onto it. Some guy gave her beloved son a well-deserved punch in the face. An unforgivable crime! However, it did give me a lead into other irregularities that I need to follow up. It also prompted me to put my boss under surveillance when he let slip he had business in Strasbourg when I asked him to our soiree last month. His office cum flat in Strasbourg is a cover. His mistress is a freelance stenographer, translator and interpreter and as such can work for Peter on legitimate business. He has a legitimate requirement for her services but his contract includes mistress. Mistresses can be brought, especially if they realise their partner will be unmasked and I intend to unmask this particular one. President Cripp will be delighted. He knows that Peter is trying to undermine Commissioner Crouton, who is vulnerable to charges of misuse of funds."

"I should have thought that that could apply equally to the profligate costs of Madame

O'Connor's so called non-paid committee work."

"True. That's another string to my bow. The whole O'Connor household is paid from commission expenses."

"Good. The thought of Clara as the President's Lady is almost too much to bear. What are you waiting for?"

"I need to keep President Cripp informed. I am also working closely with Peter on the Australian lobby. I am looking for a loophole in their legitimacy and I think I have found it. Students are bound to work at least three years in Europe after completing a government-sponsored course to prevent the brain drain. Some students manage to get through the net. By keeping in touch with Peter on this project, which is being carried out at his specific request, I can appear to be working in close collaboration with him."

"Whilst stabbing him in the back," laughed Louise.

Sally surveyed her new abode.

"Sorry it's so cramped," Fred said.

"Better than the street, darling," Sally said putting her arm round his shoulder. "It won't be for long anyway. I can't wait to get to Australia."

"It won't be before the end of the summer term; after we have graduated."

Summer seemed a long time coming.

.

CHAPTER 10

It was a beautiful Spring. The Media were taking an interest in the coming election for the next President of the Commission. They were rooting for Commissioner O'Connor, as Mr Clean. The MEPs had little option but to follow popular opinion. There was a call for Commissioner Crouton to resign over improper use of public funds. The President's continuing support for her was unpopular. Nothing it seemed could stop the O'Connor bandwagon.

Commissioner O'Connor was spending the weekend in Sussex enjoying the rare approbation of his wife.

Emille received a caller from THE EUROPEAN, the most influential magazine on the Internet.

Sally and Fred were on an Outward-Bound Sailing Course on the Clyde, having finished the spring term and with it their final year.

Enjoying a pre-lunch drink the O'Connors were watching the wall screen. A Bishop was discussing religion with an agnostic scientist. "The bible and religion outlast regimes," declared the Bishop.

"Rubbish," said John, switching over to the news programme. "The bible must die now that we understand the origins of the universe."

"Think about it more deeply, John," said his father." To begin with it is not one book. It is a collection of books, Jewish law, history, mythology, stories and parables, and the New Testament. Each generation should look at it anew. I agree with the Bishop."

John's response was cut short when the Director General of the Police Inspectorate came on the screen. He was talking about the Australian Lobby, assuring his listeners that it would soon be exposed as an illegal organisation.

"I feel a bit guilty about that," said Peter.

"Guilty? Why?" asked Clara, "isn't making Sally and her miserable little boy-friend the scapegoat just what we wanted?"

"What you wanted. Sally doesn't deserve to be set up in this way. We started something I couldn't stop. Once Poirot had latched onto a legal loophole in the Lobby and boasted about it to the President it was too late."

"Why on earth would you want to stop it?"

"I didn't know he would link the personal investigation to the Lobby. I think The President's girl-friend's foreign policy is wrong. I have some sympathy with the Australians and think we should come out in support of their position."

"What nonsense. Is that why you're so anxious to discredit the Crouton woman, insinuating her relationship with the President is more than he admits?"

A picture of Peter appeared - nothing unusual: he was often quoted on the media. There was no quote this time but a picture of Emille alongside his with the caption:

'Commissioner O'Connor's secret mistress.'

"What's this," screeched Clara.

"Good heavens," Peter spluttered. "That's my office manager. Someone's up to mischief."

"Office manager! It's the first I've heard of an office manager at your Strasbourg flat," exclaimed Clara as the details were emerging on the screen. "She's only a girl."

"That's an old photograph. She's in her mid-thirties," said Peter truthfully. "You wouldn't know of her. She's a temp' from an agency."

"What sort of agency?" grinned John. "I'd like to pay it a visit."

"Be quiet John," snapped Clara. "Peter, you had better scotch this so-called mischief right now. If you don't, don't dare set foot in this house again."

When Peter entered the Presidents office he expressed no surprise at Commissioner Crouton's presence, merely saying:

"I was hoping for a private meeting with you, Mr President. Our business is of a personal nature. It has nothing to do with Commissioner Crouton."

"As a Vice-President and now President designate it is very much the concern of Commissioner Crouton," responded the President.

"Commissioner Crouton is not President designate. I am also to be nominated."

"You don't expect nominations now that your platform of moral righteousness is in ruins do you."

"How can you say it is in ruins? The lady quoted by the Times correspondent is my perfectly legitimate office manager."

"Oh Peter," laughed Commissioner Crouton. "How can you be so naive? You are just not street wise. Haven't you learnt yet how fickle a mistress can be when money is involved?"

"I don't believe it of Emille." Peter said quietly.

Commissioner Crouton roared with laughter. "Then go and find out for yourself," she said.

Peter, enraged by Crouton's revelation headed, for his Strasbourg flat, not that he really expected to find Emille still there. To his surprise, she was there.

"You've got a nerve staying here," he blurted out. "How much did they pay you?"

Emille's slap across his face was so hard that he staggered back against the wall.

"You fool," she cried through her tear stained face. "You stupid fool. Didn't I warn you not to trust that Crouton woman, and you would listen to her rather than me. We've been under surveillance from your own damned inspectorate for six months. That reporter from the Times told me they had a whole dossier leaked to them, including full documentation of your domestic set up and staff. And yet there was a way we could have sorted it out. I hate you. I hate you. I never want to set eyes on you again."

Peter stood staring at the open door.

The flat seemed very empty.

CHAPTER 11

A new beginning?

"I feel uneasy," said Sally.

"It's only natural," said Fred. "If you have second thoughts we can still pull out."

"No, it's not that. It's all been too easy. Mrs O'Connor is not the sort of person to make empty threats, yet since I left my flat there has been nothing."

"I reckon that John's mother found out what really went on and didn't want any more to do with it," said Fred.

They were having tea, sitting in the well of the 12-metre yacht they had chartered following the successful completion of their Outward -Bound sailing course, leading to the European Yachting Association Inshore Skippers Certificate. Logging a journey to Lerwick in the Shetlands and back to the Clyde would convert it to an Offshore Certificate of Competence.

Looking up they were aware of a lady looking down at them from the marina jetty. Although it was mild she was wearing an anorak with the hood up almost obscuring her light blond hair. She had a knapsack on her back.

"May I have a word with you," she said.

Sally responded to the anxious tone of her voice. "Of course," she said. Fred stood up to hold the lady's hand as she climbed aboard.

"Thank you," she said, dropping off her knapsack and sitting down with obvious relief. She threw back her hood to reveal the face of a strikingly beautiful woman.

"You would like some tea, or perhaps coffee?" asked Sally, still wondering who this strange lady might be.

"Tea would be most refreshing," the lady answered with a trace of a foreign accent, which Sally identified as French; then she stared in horror, teapot poised in mid-air as Emille continued.

"I have come to warn you. The police-inspectorate have a file on you and your liaison with the Australian Lobby. They know your departure date for next week and where you will be met. There will be a fast Aqua-jet ready to intercept you and the transfer launch at the rendezvous. Killing two birds with one stone, as they say. Exposing the embarrassing Australian Lobby, and satisfying the vengeful Clara

O'Connor. It would be very serious for you both."

"Who are you and how do you know all this?" asked Fred.

"You obviously haven't seen the news during the last few days," said Emille. "My picture is all over the media coverage. This is what I am trying to get away from."

"No," said Sally recovering sufficiently to pour Emille her tea and pass it to her. "We came to escape the real - or perhaps I should say the unreal world. This boat doesn't even have an engine. We rely entirely on the elements, except for heat and our navigation lights, which use paraffin, so without electric power we are out of touch."

"I am, or was, the mistress and lover of Peter O'Connor. We have been exposed by the same investigation that was undertaken to expose you and the Lobby. The Director General of the Police Inspectorate kept Peter informed about the Lobby investigation; but, of-course, kept our scandal between himself and the Commission President."

"So we're finished," said Sally; collapsing back onto her seat. "The O'Connor's have won after all."

"Not necessarily," said Emille. "Peter told me all about it because he was not happy about it and regretted setting it in motion," She looked at Sally. "He didn't think you deserved the serious consequences; but the Director General of the Inspectorate had told Cripps and Crouton how the Lobby were acting illegally, by amongst other things, helping students to escape their three-year commitment; and it was too late to stop it."

"So we're finished," echoed Fred.

"You are not due to submit your sail plan to the European Yachting Association till next week," said Emille.

"Good heavens! How did you know that," exclaimed Fred.

"A copy of your file is in Peter's office. I am Peter's office manager so I had access to it The Inspectorate are working with the EYA. So my suggestion is you slip away under cover of darkness before that date, and sail direct to Reykjavik instead of waiting to rendezvous with rendezvous boat, which will still be in Iceland - probably Reykjavik"

"You've got it all worked out," said Fred, "Why your interest?"

"I want to join you," said Emille on the verge of tears. "There's nothing left for me here."

"Of course you can join us," said Sally, "and you look famished. When did you last eat?"

"Yesterday. I booked through the Tunnel to London and then hid my identity ring in metal foil in my bag. I managed to stay on the train to Glasgow. The electric cab driver was more than happy to take cash for the journey here with no questions asked."

Sally called out to Fred to lower the Radar reflector and stow it below water level as she led Emille below. "And I'll be slapping some more of that non-reflecting paint on the mast while I'm about it," Fred responded, hauling himself to the top of the mast in the boson's chair.

He soon finished the painting and was lowering the Radar reflector when he noticed a man on the jetty was watching him. His face was largely hidden by the hood of a cloak, the sort of cloak that would have been fashionable about a decade ago.

"Good afternoon," the man said in a cultured voice.

"Good afternoon," responded Fred, offering no further encouragement for a continued conversation.

The man paused. "Making preparations for your offshore venture next week?" he enquired.

"Yes," said Fred. "We've a lot to do," he added pointedly; but the man was not deterred.

"I've come to try to persuade you to abandon your plan," he said.

"Our sail plan is ready to submit to the EYA next week," Fred said. "Why should we abandon it? What business is it of yours anyway?"

"I'm not talking of your EYA plan, but of your alternative plan which was very much my business. You must be Frederick Howard."

"Who the hell are you," Fred shouted - deliberately. Emille and Sally, alerted, stood behind the cabin hatch.

"I'm Peter O'Connor, formerly Commissioner O'Connor, I've probably been stripped of that title now. I am known to your friend Sally, and came to warn her. If she stops her plan now there is nothing that can be brought against her. She has a clean record. Perhaps I can come aboard and talk to her."

"How can I trust an O'Connor?"

"You've got to believe me. My life is in ruins. I've destroyed the faith in me of the only woman I ever really loved and wanted to marry. At least I can stop ruining another life. Two lives in fact. You would be arrested alongside Sally. For your own sake you have to trust me."

"You can trust him," called Emille from the Hatch.

"Emille!" Peter O'Connor jumped into the well straight into her arms.

"Bring that Radar reflector into the cabin Fred," said Sally. "I've kept some hot soup for you."

"It's truly surprising what you two can cook up over a paraffin stove," said Peter sipping an after-dinner brandy from a plastic mug.

"I've more I can cook up yet," said Emille. In answer to their unspoken question she went on, "a recovery programme. You said you were finished just now Peter. That's out of character. You even suggested joining us to Australia. Why not stay and fight?"

"Fight? What with?"

"With me. There's nothing to grab the media headlines like a scarlet woman. It even displaces sport in the public interest; and you just watch me play the part." There was stunned silence. Emille continued. "You and I Peter have disappeared, successfully avoiding the media. Our reappearance together will give us the headlines. Crouton and Cripps won't get a look in. We can turn the situation around. Clara has always maintained that her good work was separate from and independent of your office and influence. So be it. It's the Sussex home that is under scrutiny for profligate spending, you ran a pretty tight ship from your Brussels office. To cap it all you are going to make an honest woman of this wicked lady."

"We'll fight," said Peter. "And I'll fight for a complete overhaul of the system. I'll call into question the rigidity of the system, the rigidity of the Treaties. I'll fight on a platform for overhauling the set-up from top to bottom - a new start, less utopian, more practical, more accountable." Emille caught his eye, "and," he added, "less control from the top, delegation to local areas."

"That should catch on," said Fred. "It's bold. It's the sort of approach it might be worth staying and fighting for, Sally."

"It would. We'll cancel the rendezvous, warn our friends and cancel our yacht charter. That will confound the enemy to start with.

Then we'll use our influence in the Lobby to back you. I can't wait to get started."

APPENDIX

2066 AND ALL THAT

by

One of the Common People

CONTENTS

84

BENEFICIARIES OF THE FUTURE:

1. **The politicians**, particularly the European politicians. They will be BIG in Europe, rubber stamping the diktats of the apparatchiks, enjoy a big salary with little power or responsibility. This will be a GOOD THING for the politicians.

2. **BIG BUSINESS**. They will be BIG in Europe, and the fat cats will get fatter. This will be a GOOD THING for **fat cats**

3 **Farmers**, particularly large farmers, who will get even larger. Little farmers will be buried under the weight of Euro-bureaucracy. A GOOD THING for large farmers.

4 4.**Trade Unions.** They will have the Social Contract!

5 **Terrorists, criminals, lawyers, etc.** They will have the European Court of Justice (euro-speak for Law). A GOOD THING for terrorists, criminals, lawyers, etc.

6.   The devolved states of Scotland, Wales and Northern Ireland. They may prefer becoming regions of Europe; European laws overriding their own laws. They may consider this a GOOD THING.

7.   Bureaucrats. They will become very important and increase according to the laws of Parkinson (summarised in a later section), get fat salaries and expenses, a very GOOD THING for bureaucrats.

A GOOD THING for everyone - except the common people.

2. THE PRIMARY PURPOSE OF GOVERNMENT

Ask any Member of Parliament or contemporary politician to define the primary purpose of government. It is not difficult to imagine the high moral tone of the various answers - Justice for the people, Health, Education, Human Rights, Lesbian Rights, and all sorts of other rights (no mention of responsibilities). There is probably only one or two living politicians who would mention Defence of The Realm. What price our rights under the Nazi jack-boot?

Can there any longer be any Defence of The Realm? Mrs Thatcher on Europe: "Economic and monetary union...would in effect require political union, a United States of Europe. This is not on the agenda."

Mrs Thatcher was defeated and it is on the agenda.

What is the agenda? A worms-eye view of all the common people need to know will be found in the following pages.

3.

SOVEREIGNTY

1. The Creeping Sell-out.

2. The double U-Turn.

3. The rule making machine, or the criminalisation of the common people.

1. The Creeping Sell-out.

Very few, if any, of the common people would have bothered to read The Treaty of Rome. The size and weight of the thing was sufficient to make them suspicious, and with an unerring instinct write it off as a load of ideological Humbug.

It is a matter for conjecture if any of the 'top people' read the Treaty either.

The European Communities Act of 1972 enabled directives from the Brussels law making machine to become British law, virtually unscrutinised.

Traditionally law making was the province of parliament, requiring open debate. Laws are now coming into being through the back door through recommendations, directives and various other 'Statutory Instruments.' Theoretically they are scrutinised by parliament.

In practice the sheer quantity is too great for any realistic scrutiny to take place: not that it would signify, since commission law overrides national law.

In 1975 the common people voted YES for continued membership of the COMMON-MARKET - NOT THE EUROPEAN UNION. They were told by those they trusted that this was a GOOD THING for Britain and in no-way would it affect sovereignty.

One politician had read The Treaty, and was one of the few who had had the intelligence to understand its implications. It was flawed. He had the honesty and integrity to warn the common people -he was misquoted, ridiculed and hounded out of the party. It is still not politically correct to say Enoch Powell was right!

2. The Double U-Turn.

The opposition party of the day called for a NO vote on the referendum called to decide whether or not we should join the common market - because the other side were saying YES.

Strange, that when the opposition came into power as New Labour they became ardent Europhiles. It was for the younger members of the new opposition to point out the dangers of European domination. Are these U turns due to genuine conviction, or is it party loyalty before patriotic duty. The true split as seen by the common people has nothing to do with party; but between those in both parties, or no party at all, who believe membership of the European Union is a GOOD THING and those who believe it is a BAD THING.

As early as 1964, well before the referendum the matter of sovereignty was clearly stated. In a case before the European Court, namely Costa v Enel, the Court stated that the Treaty of Rome "comes with it a permanent limitation of sovereign rights." So there it is. Let there be no more weasel words. Member states (previously known as countries) are subject to the overriding laws of the European Union.

English and Scottish laws that have been honed and tested over hundreds of years can be overturned at a stroke by the application of bureaucratic edicts emanating from laws enacted by the European Parliament/Commission:

"It follows from this that Community law which was enacted in accordance with the powers laid down in the treaties, has priority over any conflicting law of the Member States. Not only is it stronger than earlier national law, but it also has a limiting effect on laws adopted subsequently."

3. The Rule Making Machine, or 20,000 ways of becoming a criminal.

Article 189(2)EC specifically states that a regulation is `directly applicable to all Member States.' Regulations are only one of the tools whereby community law impacts on national law. There are also Directives, Decisions, Recommendations, and Opinions; the subtle differences between these need not concern the common people - the European Court of Justice (Euro-speak for Law) ensures that contravention of any of them will invariably mean that the EU rules; "...for," quotes the Dr Klaus-Dieter Borchardt, "...what would remain of the Community legal order if Community law were to be subordinated to national law? ...the construction of a united Europe on which so many hopes rest would never be achieved." Who's hopes? Has nothing been learned from history of the fate of people living in totalitarian states - the people shall have freedom; the people shall have rights; there shall be harmonisation, so long, of course that their freedom and rights don't get in the way of "harmonisation."

.   In the name of harmonisation, liberalisation and other similar buzz words there are over 20,000 ways in which the common people can be made criminals, whether they be producing honey, growing `non-harmonised' tomatoes in their back garden and selling them, or indeed carrying on with their business in the same way as they had, without interference, for centuries. Nor has the stream stopped: there is a continuous outpouring of legislation.   The European Union's A GUIDE FOR STUDENTS AND TEACHERS would have us believe, agreed by our national Ministers! Typically:

Commission   decision   "94/924, establishing the ecological criteria for the award of the Community eco-label for toilet paper."

"3945/89 Commission Regulation fixing certain indicative ceilings and additional detailed rules for the application of the supplementary trade mechanisms to fruit and vegetables, as regards broad-leaved endives.

Traders in broad-leaved endives beware!

Be careful if you are selling nectarines. In June, 1995 it was reported that a fruit merchant from Hull was told that it would be a criminal offence to sell his nectarines because they were too small. The fact that housewives might be quite happy to buy them (they could have more taste) was of no consequence. It was decreed that housewives had no say in such matters. Community Law protects the consumer. Officials have much more experience of what is good for the consumer. No doubt they advise their wives accordingly when out doing the weekend shopping.

At this point it must be remembered that some of the rule making apparatchiks will be females of the species. In such cases their husbands can rest assured fruit and veg purchased by them is compatible with the relevant EC requirements.

The commercial growers will have made sure that they had not wasted their registration fees to harmonise any product, however tasty, that will not give them the most economical return, thus protecting the consumer from making difficult choices - or something like that.

To administer and supervise this mass of centralised planning an army of bureaucrats and officials are created and armed with a mountain of regulations that can criminalise almost any activity, however apparently innocent, that activity might appear.

4. Two Cod wars:

"We live in an island sitting on coal and surrounded by fish."
Attributed to Aneurin Bevan.

When the officials of DG XIV (whatever that is) in Brussels set out their quota system outlining the tonnage of each species of fish various countries would be allowed to catch in Community waters, they neglected to tell the fish. Thus, the fish knew as much about the quota system as the officials knew about fishing, and insisted on swimming into the wrong nets. This causes a greater conservation and ecological disaster than the officials were seeking to avoid.

The fish would also be blissfully ignorant of the two cod wars that were fought for their possession.

The first was Iceland fighting what had been the greatest maritime nation on earth to defend the fish stocks in her territorial waters from encroachment by foreign fishing vessels.

Iceland won this war. By international law all countries could extend their fishing limits to two hundred miles, or where the coast lines of two countries were closer, to the median line between them.

The second cod-war is never acknowledged since it was lost before it began, with but a whimper of protest. In accordance with international law the British parliament passed the Fisheries Limits Act extending Britons limit to the 200 miles allowed by international law; but not by European law. The British act of parliament was overruled by Council Regulation 2141/70, reissued as regulation 101/76, which stated that all member states had the right of equal access to all fishing waters under British jurisdiction!

The massive fishing fleets of Spain and other European countries have almost fished our waters dry. 'Fresh Icelandic fish' the supermarkets proudly proclaim!

NOTE: There has been updates on fishing regulations, but they are still dependent on the diktats of the EU.

5. Inward investment:

Was it a BAD THING when earlier in the 20th century William Morris built up Morris Motors from scratch.   Henry Royce built prestige cars, one at a time, later to be joined by Charles Rolls to form the Rolls-Royce company, De-Haviland, A.V.Roe, Sopwith and others built up our aircraft industry, arguably, during the war, the best in the world. The first commercial television broadcasts were made in the UK with equipment developed initially by John Logie Baird, followed by EMI/Marconi.   Now the majority of television receivers are supplied by foreign manufacturers.   Railways around the world, were the offspring of James Watt and Stevenson's 'Rocket.'

When Marconi wished to exploit the propagation of radio waves for commercial purposes, fathering today's Information Technology industry, it was to this country that he came; in similar circumstances today, he would go "some-place else."

Radar, one of the few new technologies initiated by the government, instigated by Sir Robert Watson-Watt (of the scientific civil service) and encouraged by Churchill in the thirties, was developed at Orford-ness and Bawdsey Manor, Suffolk; known originally as

RDF (Radio Direction Finding) when it contributed to the success of "The Battle of Britain" and defeat of the U-boats. This may surprise the Americans, who later invented the name Radar. One could go on!

Even the binary Boolean logic and radio propagation used for the language and propagation of data on the internet owe there beginnings to Clerk Maxwell and George Boole

New Britain has a new outlook, looking for new Inward Investment.

5. PARKINSON'S LAW REVISITED

> "...and I recall one low point when nine Foreign Ministers from the major countries of Europe solemnly assembled in Brussels to spend several hours discussing how to resolve their differences on standardising a fixed position of rear-view mirrors on agricultural tractors."
>
> James Callaghan.

It is doubtful if any of the apparatchiks of Brussels, or even Westminster have read the treatise of Professor C. Northcote Parkinson, first published in the U.K. in 1958 by John Murray, priced three shillings and sixpence. Any such as may have come across it would find its truisms so unpalatable that they would hurriedly tuck it away at the bottom of their filing cabinet and try to forget it. For no-matter how many laws emanate from the bureaucratic machinery, it is Parkinson's Law that ultimately prevails. The greater the bureaucracy and the more rigid the law the more relevant are the laws according to Parkinson. For all his astute-

perception the professor could not have envisaged the burgeoning application of his laws to their present extent, or the enthusiasm for extending them further.

A review of the main tenets of his treaty may be relevant. The full text of his work may be found gathering dust in most public libraries.

His first law, "work expands to fill the time available," he follows with his equation showing that in any bureaucratic organisation there is an average increase in bureaucratic staff of 6.56 per cent per annum - irrespective of work load.

Historical examples are:

1.   2000 admiralty officials in 1914 increased to 3559 in 1928, whist the numbers of fighting men diminished by a third and the number of ships by two thirds!

2.   The colonial staff increased from 373 in 1935 to 1,661 in 1954 at a time when the colonies had virtually ceased to exist

THE LAW OF TRIVIALITY

The Law of Triviality states that the time spent in committee on any item will be inversely proportional to its cost - or complexity.

Parkinson cites the prolonged discussions relating to the building of a cycle shed for use of the staff, which is easy to understand and waffle on about at length, as opposed to a proposal and quote for a reactor, at a cost of several million, which is a sum that is outside the personal experience of those comprising the committee and has only a notional meaning; thus will be cleared, give or take a million or two, by accepting an outside contractor's advice with, a minimum of discussion.

Finally, the cost of supplying coffee and biscuits for the meetings at an annual cost of £21.50 is considered extortionate, requiring a lengthy argument as to whether it is really justified and a request that details of the expenditure be supplied for further consideration at the next meeting.

Of course, the above examples are entirely fictitious. Nothing like that could possibly happen at discussions at the heart of Europe.

Mrs Thatcher noted in her memoirs, The Downing Street Years, "The ability of those present (at the Inter-Governmental Conference of December 1985) to argue at great length and with much repetition about matters of little interest was, as ever, astonishing."

COMMITTOLOGY

Parkinson's Co-efficient of Inefficiency really needs reference to the original work. Suffice it to say here that he has reached a conditional conclusion that the optimum number for any committee is eight. The point of ineffectiveness is reached when the numbers exceed twenty-one. However, in that in any committee the law of triviality prevails, the membership is irrelevant.

There is an overriding codicil to the above. It may be defined as the pre-meeting meetings effect, whereby a group decides the outcome of a meeting before it starts; or where, particularly at ministerial meetings, the officials set the agenda and define the outcome before the meeting and advise the participants - or selected participants - accordingly.

It must be said for the apparatchiks of Europe, that they understand the main precepts of "comitology" perfectly and use them with great skill. Mrs Thatcher, while fighting courageously to attempt to inject a little common sense and reality into the Common Market, recorded in her memoirs, The Downing Street Years: "What I did not know that behind the scenes the Italians had agreed with a proposal emanating from Germany and endorsed by Christian Democratic leaders from several European countries at an earlier caucus meeting..."

PARKINSON'S ADMINISTRATIVE BLOCK

"For years it has been
my job to promote unity
amongst conflicting
organisations and I would
never have succeeded if I had
put before them cut and dried
constitutions."
Earnest Bevin,
speaking of the
League of Nations in
1939

What a pity ideologists don't look back in history before embarking on their dream world. Consider the history of great buildings.

What a wonderful idea The League of Nations was; set up to end all wars. A purpose-built building, The Palace of Nations to house the League, having all the facilities required, was completed and opened in 1937 - just two years before the Second World War!

There is now a magnificent edifice, a purpose built parliamentary building with all the facilities for MEPs, their secretaries, advisers, consultants, conferencing, etc.

Let Parkinson have the last word. "Examples abound of new institutions coming into existence with an establishment of executives, consultants etc. in a building specially designed for their purpose. Experience proves that such a building will die. ...**It cannot grow naturally, for it is already grown.** When we see an example of such planning ...the experts among us shake their heads sadly, draw a sheet over the corpse, and tiptoe quietly away."

Conclusions:

It might be thought reading the above observations that the conclusion was to be "Let's get out of Here." Not necessarily so; the Mother of Parliaments evolved over centuries, originally without a commoner's vote; but, is it perfect? To quote Churchill: "Democracy is a terrible form of government, but it is the best there is."

In these uncertain and changing times it may be "Better to Stick Together." Perhaps the EU, given time (a few centuries), will throw off some the above observed autocratic imperfections!

Reference to section 5 above indicates the potential of the people of Great Britain. The younger generation showed their metal at the Olympics at Rio. They still have that potential!